The Missing Link on
Mary Lincoln

The Missing Link on *Mary Lincoln*

ANNE G. SNOW

iUniverse LLC
Bloomington

The Missing Link on Mary Lincoln

Cover Illustration
Scott M. Snow

iUniverse books may be ordered through booksellers or by contacting:

iUniverse LLC
1663 Liberty Drive
Bloomington, IN 47403
www.iuniverse.com
1-800-Authors (1-800-288-4677)

ISBN: 978-1-4620-4105-3 (sc)
ISBN: 978-1-4620-4106-0 (e)

Printed in the United States of America

iUniverse rev. date: 11/25/2013

AUTHOR'S NOTES

THE MISSING LINK ON MARY LINCOLN was written for school children, their teachers and parents, who have been exposed to many books with untrue and negative accounts about Mary Todd Lincoln, wife of our 16th President, Abraham Lincoln. I wrote this book over fifty years ago as a Fifth Grade teacher who loved teaching American History. When I taught about the Civil War, I was determined to tell the truth about Mary Lincoln. The school library books did not reveal that these two great minds had so much in common, and that Mary was Lincoln's only true love. Many books gave the impression that Lincoln was a melancholy boy brought up in poverty and even pining over the death of a sweetheart. I learned that these assumptions were wrong after personal research and especially after reading a 1953 published book by Ruth Painter Randall: **MARY LINCOLN** _Biography of a Marriage_ Little, Brown & Company.

The result of Mrs. Randall's researches is "a biography which answers once and for all, the charges leveled against Mary Lincoln for [now]' nearly a hundred and fifty years."

It was a revelation to read many stories of Mary Todd and Abraham Lincoln's courtship and marriage, truly one of the greatest love stories in our nation's history. They demonstrated love and affection for each other and for their sons that was uncommon in that day. Mrs. Randall reveals "for the first time—the truth about one of the most controversial women in American history, and the never-before-told, never-to-be-forgotten story of her life with Abraham Lincoln."

Refer to the APPENDIX for more information on Ruth Painter Randall, for whom this book is dedicated. Read the quote from Carl Sandberg, a noted Lincoln author whose statement in part:

"It can stand as the first and most indispensable book to be read by those seeking to know of the Lincoln couple . . . "

More books have been written about Lincoln than any other president or famous American. I have read at least "four score and seven" of them . . . including many children's books, to feel qualified to write yet another. This latest edit introduces children to the book, but advances to a reading level directed to parents and teachers as they share it with children. Because of the controversy created and gossip printed by authors and newspapers in the past, many adults feel and express a negative impression of Mary Lincoln., This book portrays an educated, intelligent woman and shows her true character. She deserves a place of respect in the annals of American history.

In easy to read large font, this story covers the main facts about Mary and Abe from their births to their deaths. Credits are given for the many famous and familiar photographs that can be found in an indefinite number of books.

This notable year, 2009 when Americans celebrate _TWO HUNDRED_ years since President Abraham Lincoln was born, February 12, 1809, is a good time to add truth and honor to the name of his wife, Mary Todd Lincoln.

ANNE G. SNOW

© 2009

dedicated to

RUTH PAINTER RANDALL

for her kind and understanding story
of the lives of

Mary Todd Lincoln

and

President Abraham Lincoln

A friend of Abraham Lincoln said, "I chatted with the First Lady in the great East
Room one evening and noticed that Lincoln looked often at his wife.
At length President Lincoln laughed pleasantly and said,
"My wife is as handsome as when she was a girl, and I, a poor nobody then, fell
in love with her; and what is more I have never fallen out."

This is the story of a "First Lady."
We call the wife of the President of the United States "First Lady."
This lady was the wife of President Lincoln.
Everyone knows about Abraham Lincoln, our 16th President.
But everyone doesn't know the truth about his wife,
Mary Todd Lincoln.

LOG CABIN

A replica of Lincoln's birthplace.

From a log cabin to the White House. A replica of Lincoln's Kentucky birthplace.

Abraham Lincoln was born in a small log cabin on a Kentucky farm
to Thomas and Nancy Lincoln on February 12, 1809.
Many people believe that because Lincoln was born in
a log cabin, he grew up in poverty.
But many families lived in log cabins in the early 1800's.
Abe and his sister Sarah were well-fed and well-clothed.

When Abe was only seven years old his father, Thomas Lincoln, decided to buy 160 acres of forest land in Indiana, where slavery was not practiced. This attracted Mr. Lincoln because he didn't believe slavery was right. Abe's father was a rugged pioneer, who, like many other Americans, wasn't afraid of moving west and settling new lands. So he loaded his belongings into a wagon, and with Nancy, his wife, and his two children Sarah and Abraham, they moved to that state. Abe was big for his age and worked hard with his father to clear the land to make a farm.

MANSION

The wealthy Robert Todd family lived in this lovely home with stately trees and a fan shaped window over the front door in the beautiful town of Lexington, Kentucky.

There was great happiness in this home on
December 13, 1818 when
Eliza Parker Todd gave birth to the couple's third child,
a beautiful baby girl they named Mary.

Mr. Todd provided well for his family. Mary had horses to ride and a carriage to take her wherever she wanted to go. Her household included many slaves whom Mary considered beloved members of the family.

SADNESS

That same year when Mary Todd was born, Abe was nine years old. There was much sadness in the Lincoln home because his loving mother, Nancy Hanks Lincoln, died.

However, a few years later, Mary was to experience the same grief that Abe was going through. She was only seven years old when her mother and baby sister both died. Feeling lost and frightened, Mary cried with her older sisters Elizabeth and Frances and her younger sister Ann. Her father and two brothers, Levi and George, were also very sad.

The four household slaves tried to comfort the Todd family. Old Nelson shed big tears as he stood by in his blue swallowtail coat adorned with large brass buttons. It was Mary's "Mammy Sally" who held her in her arms and gave her comfort.

STEPMOTHERS FOR ABE AND MARY

Abe's father was soon married again to a kind widow, Sarah Johnston.
She had three children of her own.

Abe's stepmother stimulated his interest in reading and learning. She encouraged his natural sense of humor. The arrival of his stepmother was a turning point in ten-year-old Abraham's life. Not only did she bring with her an amazing collection of household items: a feather bed, a walnut dresser a table and chairs, knives, forks and spoons, and a spinning wheel, but she also brought her children: Elizabeth (thirteen), John D. (ten), and Matilda (eight). These lively youngsters put laughter back into the lonely Lincoln cabin.

Next his stepmother turned her attention to the cabin, insisting Thomas finish the roof and put in a wooden floor. She had her new husband cover the windows with greased paper, build an upstairs loft for the boys, and make decent beds for all eight of the family members, counting Abe's cousin Dennis Hanks, who at nineteen years of age had come to live with the Lincolns after Nancy died.

Sarah and Thomas had no children together, but Abe's new mother managed to blend the two families into one. She loved Thomas's children, and grew especially fond of Abraham.

Mary's father also married again. Mary's new mother was Elizabeth Humphreys, a young, pretty lady with no children. She believed in strict rules and expected her six step-children to be quiet and obedient. Nine more children were born into the Todd family. The new mother had so many children that she did not want to be bothered with six stepchildren.

In spite of all the restrictions, and the lack of understanding between Mary and her stepmother, her days as a little girl were happy. Living in a big house with servants, and eating meals around a long table with a big family of children was fun, especially because the children around that table were keen-witted, spunky, and teasing young Todds.

MARY TODD ATTENDED GOOD SCHOOLS AND WAS WELL EDUCATED

Mary's father, a successful banker, was able to send Mary and her sisters to Mr. Ward's Academy within walking distance of their house. They had lots of homework and even an early morning French class at 5:00 a.m. Mary was very bright and learned her lessons well, in fact, faster than her classmates.

Robert Todd could see that his daughter needed more challenges in her education. One night he announced to the whole family, "Before long Mary will be a young lady. Ma and I have decided to send her to a finishing school—Madame Mentelle's boarding school."

Mary had dreamed of going to a boarding school, especially one like this. She was taught by Madame Mentelle and her husband who had escaped from France during the French Revolution.

Mary Todd loved to act. She had the leading part in many dramas presented at Madame Mentelle's school. She was even assigned to write a play in French. After four years of studying the language, she spoke it fluently.

Perhaps the most important things Mary learned were good manners and all the acceptable graces for the socials and parties of that day. She learned to welcome people graciously and to be interested in them.

Since the family was prosperous, the Todd daughters always had stylish clothes. Mary grew up loving pretty things and had many lovely dresses to wear.

Mary also loved books and had many to read. The Todd library was filled with fine leather-bound books, including all the classics Mary studied in the schools she attended.

ABE LINCOLN WAS WELL-READ AND WELL EDUCATED.

Abe Lincoln loved books too. Family members recalled him as always having one in his hand, or in his pocket, always reading in the day or by firelight at night. Good books were scarce on the frontier. Other than Abe's classroom texts, his first books were those that Sarah Lincoln had brought with her from Kentucky. One was the family Bible. Some of the others were The Pilgrims Progress, Robinson Crusoe, and a biography of George Washington.

Nighttime, by the light of a flickering fire, long after others in his family had gone to bed, was Abe's favorite time to read.—Stories from the Bible, stories from *Weems' Life of Washington,* and *Pilgrims Progress.* He read them over and over again. Any book he could get his hands on was a treasure to him.

He said his schooling was in bits and pieces over the years while he attended any country school available and worked hard on his father's farms, splitting rails. Abraham reached his full height of 6 feet 4 inches long before he was 20 years old. Even as a boy, Lincoln showed ability as a speaker. He could keep any group of people around him spellbound as he discussed news or problems of the day. Young Abe Lincoln was a great communicator. He could remember what he had read and repeat it to young boys and even adults as he associated with them. Once he imitated a preacher and got lots of laughs from the young men, but not from the preacher.

"In 1823, when Abraham was 14, his parents joined the Pigeon Creek Baptist Church. There was bitter rivalry among Baptists, Methodist, Presbyterians, and members of other denominations. Young Lincoln disliked any display of bitterness among Christian people. This may explain why he never joined any Church, and why he never attended church regularly. Yet, he became a man of deep religious feelings. The Bible was one of the few books his parents owned. Abraham came to know it thoroughly."

[World Book encyclopedia, 1964]

HENRY CLAY
A FRIEND OF MARY'S FATHER
AND ALSO OF YOUNG MARY

Ashland home of Henry Clay. Mary left her horse tethered to a tree.

Henry Clay, a tall, important man, was a good friend to Mary's father. She had known him since the days when as a young girl, she'd ride her pony, "Snowball", down the main street of Lexington, Kentucky that led to Ashland where Mr. Clay lived. She often visited him (unannounced) but being his good friend Robert Todd's daughter, he always welcomed her even though his visits home were spaced around being a representative in Congress, even the Speaker in the House of Representatives.

Henry Clay was very vocal about his opposition to slavery. Mary loved talking to him. Mr. Clay said all the slaves should be set free. Mary herself agreed because she was hearing of terrible things that other slave owners were doing to their slaves. They were even selling them!

"I love them all!" cried Mary passionately. "I would feel as if I were selling a member of my own family."

Mary's dear Grandmother Humphreys who lived next door, believed like Mr. Clay, which explains why Mary herself shared this opinion.

OLD ENOUGH TO LEAVE HOME

When Lincoln was 21, he was free to strike out for himself but instead he stayed with his father for one more year to help him plant the first crop in Illinois where the Lincolns moved to a settlement on the north bank of the Sangamon River. He split rails for a cabin and fences. He also worked for neighboring settlers during the winter.

In the spring of 1831, when the streams were high, a trader named Denton Offutt hired Lincoln and two other young men to take a flatboat to New Orleans. Lanky Lincoln made a good impression on Offutt and was soon hired as a clerk in the man's store in New Salem, Illinois, twenty miles northwest of Springfield.

The Black Hawk War started later that year. When the Governor called out the militia, Lincoln volunteered for service. His comrades liked his friendliness, his honesty, and his skill at storytelling. They elected him Captain of the New Salem unit.

Abraham was involved in many odd jobs, such as post master and running stores for men who went out of business and left debts. Abe felt he owed them for opportunities he had. It took a long time but Abraham Lincoln paid all their debts. Because of his integrity the people he associated with called him "Honest Abe."

ABRAHAM LINCOLN GETS INTO POLITICS

"Honest Abe's" desire to do the right thing, led him to enter Politics and run for the state legislature. He served four successive two-year terms in the lower house of the Illinois General Assembly. Lincoln quickly came to the forefront in the legislature. He was witty and ready in debate. His skill in party management enabled him to become the Whig floor leader at the beginning of his second term. He took a leading part in the adoption of a plan for a system of railroads and canals and also led a successful campaign for moving the state capital from Vandalia to Springfield.

In 1834, during Lincoln's second campaign for the legislature, John T. Stuart urged him to study law. Stuart was an attorney in Springfield and a member of the legislature. Lincoln overcame his doubts about his education. He borrowed law books from Stuart and studied them. Hungry for more, he sometimes walked 20 miles from New Salem to Springfield to read books on legal law. It was customary in those days for a person to study law on his own and pass a test to become a lawyer. There were few law schools in Lincoln's time. Most lawyers simply "read law" in the office of an attorney. Abraham Lincoln studied diligently and associated with many lawyers before he took and passed the exam that would qualify him to be one of them. Abraham Lincoln received his license to practice law on September 9, 1836.

He decided to try his fortunes and begin his practice in the new state capital. Carrying all he owned in his saddle bags, he rode into Springfield in April 1837.

In Springfield he became the junior partner in the law firm of Stuart and Lincoln. Much of his time was spent traveling the circuit courts in Illinois, while he maintained an office in Springfield. Because of his eloquent and persuasive speaking ability, Lincoln influenced many people to be fair and honest.

MARY'S OLDER SISTER ELIZABETH MARRIES

Meanwhile when Mary was 13 years old, her older sister, Elizabeth, announced that she would marry Ninian Wirt Edwards, in February of 1832. Mr. Edwards was a man from way out west in Illinois. His father had been the governor of Illinois twice. Elizabeth's wedding was a grand occasion at the Todd home. All the friends and relatives filled the house. Mary was in her glory as Ma had allowed her to catch up her hair in a cascade of curls on her neck. The blue velvet dress she wore reflected the blue of her eyes as she greeted many guests at this first wedding in their family.

MARY BECOMES OLD ENOUGH TO LEAVE HOME

It was when Mary was 21 that she left home to go to Springfield, Illinois, to live with her sister Elizabeth and her husband. Mary's sister, Frances, had gone to live with the Edwards and had met a young doctor there and married him. Mary was pleased to find out that there were no slaves in Illinois. People managed to take care of their homes and families without exploiting others.

Springfield seemed to have more excitement than Mary's hometown. It had just become the state capital of Illinois. Springfield was filled with young people. There was much interest among the young men to meet and court the attractive new girl in town. One night Mary went to a dance at a big hotel in Springfield. Here, she was introduced to a Mr. Lincoln, a young lawyer and legislator, already elected to the state legislature. Mary looked at this gentleman's face. She saw dark, unruly hair, strong, rugged features, and a pair of deep-set gray eyes gazing back at her with great interest.

Mr. Lincoln was a bit shy and ill at ease, but he couldn't resist asking the pretty girl with bright chestnut hair and beautiful long lashes over blue eyes to dance with him.

"Miss Todd," he said, "I want to dance with you in the worst way."

Mary used to laugh when she told this story in later years and she'd say at the end, "and he surely did dance with me in the worst way." She remembered the 6 foot 4 inch Mr. Lincoln standing a whole foot taller than her and dancing awkwardly. Nevertheless, it was a thrill to be held in his arms and to gaze up into his eyes.

"I WAS ATTRACTED TO HER AT ONCE."

Mary and Abe were both deep thinkers and enjoyed talking together. He was attracted to her because she could talk about many things intelligently. They shared ideas about many of the books they both had read. Abe liked how Mary laughed at the things he said. He liked to see her dimples when she smiled. Her hand seemed very small and white against his great brown fist.

What a thrill when Mary learned that Abraham's political idol was her own Henry Clay.

Mary's sister Elizabeth watched Mr. Lincoln as he came to call on Mary. She noticed he sat there gazing at her, charmed, fascinated with Mary's wit and culture. Abe Lincoln was a man falling in love.

"I was attracted to her at once. The sunshine in her heart reflected in her face," are the words Lincoln wrote to a friend.

Miss Todd had many beaus, but Mr. Lincoln didn't let that stop him. He asked her to marry him and Mary vowed she would.

Because Mary lived with her sister and husband, they felt responsible for her. They thought Lincoln was beneath her class and tried to change Mary's mind about marrying him. Abe felt hurt. He wondered if they were right. They broke their engagement.

They were so miserable apart that a friend arranged for them to meet again. Overjoyed at being together, they declared nothing would part them again. They planned a wedding to take place very soon. Lincoln had already bought a gold wedding band for Mary. He even had it engraved.

The Edwards could see the great love Abe and Mary had for each other, that nothing would stop their marriage. They insisted the wedding take place in their home, instead of another place they had planned.

It was a rainy November 4, 1842, when 23 year-old Mary, looking lovely in a beautiful white wedding gown, and 33 year-old Abe, tall and serious, took their wedding vows. The joy in their hearts reflected in their eyes and in the gold ring Abe put on Mary's finger. It was inscribed "Love is Eternal."

Delighted guests shared the wedding cake still warm from being baked that day.

ABRAHAM AND MARY'S FIRST HOME

An upstairs apartment over the Globe Tavern in downtown Springfield, Illinois, was the new Mr. & Mrs. Lincoln's home the first year of their marriage. These were much simpler surroundings than Mary was accustomed to, but she worked hard and saved to help Abe get out of debt.

Each day Mary couldn't wait to greet her husband on his return from work. Abe told her about his day in the circuit courts or his law office and she shared with him the interesting things she had done that day. It was a sweet, new experience to a man who had known much loneliness. Many books quote a famous quip that Abraham Lincoln wrote in a letter to a friend a week after his marriage:

**"Nothing new here except my marrying,
which to me is a matter of profound wonder."**

A month into the marriage, Mary was excited to tell her husband of her presence in the Federal courtroom in Springfield with many of her women friends to witness "the pun of the century."

It is best told as quoted from Ruth Painter Randall's book, [pg. 77]: ". . . a glimpse of the new Mrs. Lincoln under most entertaining circumstances a month following her wedding to her beloved Abe:

"There was intense feeling against the Mormons in Illinois, and in December 1842 their prophet Joseph Smith was arrested by order of Governor Ford. A habeas corpus proceeding having been instituted to have the famous prisoner released, a hearing was conducted in the Federal courtroom in Springfield, with the town folk assembled to see the show. The judge was Nathaniel Pope, Smith's counsel was Justin Butterfield, and the picturesque scene was enhanced by the presence of the prophet's twelve Apostles. Because of the crowding, several ladies, Mary Lincoln among them, were seated on either side of the judge. Mr. Butterfield . . . rose with dignity, and amidst the most profound silence. Giving an admiring glance to the pretty women surrounding the judge and pausing a moment for oratorical effect, he delivered himself of the pun of a century:

"May it please the Court, I appear before you today under circumstances most novel and peculiar. I am to address the 'Pope' (bowing to the Judge) surrounded by angels, (bowing still lower to the ladies) in the presence of the holy Apostles, [bowing to the jury] in behalf of the Prophet of the Lord."

NEWLYWEDS

Mary's husband arrived home early that evening and they tenderly embraced as Mary asked Abe what he had done that day.

"Thought of you all day," was his answer. "What about you? How did things go in the Federal Court?"

"You'll never believe it," she answered, anxious to share her experiences there.

Abraham was all ears as his beloved wife described the "pun" she had witnessed in the trial that day. Abraham laughed and hugged her tighter as she told the story. He smiled at her animated summary of the court proceedings and the verdict—to release the prisoner.

A PARTY FOR ABE'S BIRTHDAY

Mary delighted in giving parties and sharing fun times with friends. So when her husband's birthday rolled around on February 12th, she gave the best party of their first year together.

The jovial group joined in as Mary led a "Happy Birthday toast" to Abe, "I am so glad you have a birthday. I feel so grateful to your mother."

Mary was a gracious hostess. She held the roomful of people in rapt attention. She loved people, was intensely sociable, happy and had a smile for everybody. Many years later a gentleman described her qualities in words that apply here: "I found her sympathetic, cordial, sensible, intelligent, and brimming with that good-natured friendliness so fascinating to women of the south."

A BABY

By spring Mary started sewing baby clothes. They were very long, for it was the style then for babies, like their mothers, to wear very long gowns. Mary and Abe were excited to have a child of their own.

A little boy was born to them in August. Mary wrote, "My darling husband was bending over me with much love and tenderness when that babe was born." They were full of joy and happiness at the miracle of their own child.

They named this boy Robert Todd Lincoln after Mary's father. The proud grandfather made the long hard trip from Lexington, Kentucky to Springfield to see his new grandson and namesake.

Now that they had a baby, they wanted a home of their own. They chose a cottage which was a story and a half high on Eighth Street. Mary loved this home. She worked hard cooking three meals a day on an iron stove with a wood fire. There was no running water in the kitchen, but there was a pump in the back yard near the kitchen door. It took lots of water for cooking and washing clothes and dishes and even more for bathing and for caring for that sweet baby boy, whose nickname was Bobbie.

There were oil lamps to be filled and polished. There was black Illinois mud tracked in from Springfield's unpaved streets to be washed up with soap Mary made herself. She didn't enjoy drudgery, but she delighted in making her home pretty and attractive. Any new furnishing or decoration gave her a thrill. Mr. Lincoln was becoming more prominent and she wanted to have a nice home to entertain his important friends.

At the end of the day Mary would watch for her husband to come home for supper. When she finally spied the tall figure wearing a tall hat, she would run to meet him at their gate, slip her hand in his, and swinging their hands together they would walk to the front door and enter.

ANOTHER BABY

When Bobbie was in his third year, Mary again took out the little baby clothes.

Another little boy was born to them in March 1846. They named him Edward Baker Lincoln after a dear friend. They began calling him little Eddie.

The year after Eddie's birth, Mr. Lincoln was elected to the Congress of the United States. He was to go to Washington and take his seat as a member of the House of Representatives in the nation's capital.

Mary gave a party for Abe and invited all his friends to their lovely home. Her face beamed with pride and pleasure as people praised her husband and his good works. Mary laughingly agreed and said: "He is to be President of the United States some day." She was joking, but she knew her husband was smart enough to even be the President.

EARLIEST KNOWN PICTURES OF
MR. AND MRS. LINCOLN

The Lincoln by courtesy of Library of Congress; the one of Mrs. Lincoln through the kindness of William H. Townsend

Before the family left for Washington, a Frenchman named Daguerre came to town taking pictures, a wonderful new invention where you would sit very still in front of an apparatus for a long time, and like "magic" it would create your picture.

"What will they invent next?" exclaimed Mary after she and Abe sat like statues.

Pictures made with this new method were called "daguerreotypes."

These were the Lincolns' first photographs.

TRAINS WERE INVENTED

The train was invented by then, too. People liked traveling this way better than the slow and dusty ride by horse and buggy.

Mary, Mr. Lincoln and their two lively sons traveled by train to Washington, going by way of Lexington, so Mary could visit her family home and see her father and stepmother. How all her half-brothers and sisters had grown in the eight years since she had left Kentucky! The Lincolns were excited to arrive in Washington; they had never been to the famous capital city. They enjoyed their life there: all the hustle and bustle, the social events, and the big parks.

Mr. Lincoln served in the House of Representative one term. In 1849, he and his family returned once again to their beloved home in Illinois. Abe was content with his law practice in Springfield and lost interest in politics for a while. As for Mary, she was just happy to be home with her dear husband and precious little sons, wherever that home happened to be.

GREAT SORROW

In 1849, Mary's beloved father, Robert Smith Todd was suddenly stricken with cholera and passed away. News of his death could not have reached Mary and Abraham at a worse time. Four-year-old Eddie was desperately ill and they could not leave his bedside. Mary became frantic when his condition worsened. Dear little Eddie was sick for a whole month, being checked by doctors constantly. When he died on February 1, 1850, Mary simply couldn't face this heartbreaking tragedy. She could not stop crying; she would not eat or sleep.

Abraham, haggard and grieving himself, bent over her pleading, "Eat, Mary, for we must live."

The shock of losing little Eddie left Mary nervous and hysterical, but knowing her husband and son Bobbie needed her gave her the courage to take up normal life again.

RENEWED HAPPINESS

The Lincolns were happy again when in the last month of that year another baby boy was born to them on December 21, 1850. They named him William Wallace after Mary's brother-in-law, Dr. Wallace. "Willie" was his nickname.

The year 1851 started a happier period for the Lincolns after all their sorrow. Home life was sweet and interesting for the Lincolns again. Willie was an adorable baby who looked like his mother, but had the disposition of his father.

Mary and Abe Lincoln were loving parents and could not endure the idea of spanking their children. They said the boys never required it. But some people said they were spoiling their boys because they never whipped them.

"A gentle, loving word was sufficient discipline for them." Mr. Lincoln said, "Love is the chain whereby to bind a child to its parents."

Abe and Mary let their children have fun and get into mischief. They thought their boys were wonderful, no matter what they did.

THE LINCOLNS HOPED FOR A GIRL

As enjoyable as the boys were, they wanted a little girl, too. Mary thought it would be so nice to have a little girl to fuss over and dress up in beautiful dresses. By the time Willie's second birthday came around the Lincolns knew they were to have another baby. Surely this time it would be a little girl. Mr. Lincoln had his heart set on it quite as much as Mary. He talked so much about it to some close friends who were traveling with him on the law circuit that they feared he would not be prepared to accept it if this child was another boy.

On April 4, 1853, another son was born to them. Mr. Lincoln said he should have been born on April Fools Day, because it was a big joke to them that they did not get a daughter. But the happy parents forgot all about wanting a girl when they held this healthy fourth little son in their arms. They named him Thomas after Mr. Lincoln's humble pioneer father, who had died two years before. His nickname was Tad. He and Willie grew into two bright, lively, mischievous, affectionate little boys. Willie was a handsome lad and he showed more and more of his father's qualities. Tad had dark hair and eyes like his father. He also had a very expressive face and his mother's quick, excitable disposition. The little brothers were inseparable. When Mary had to be gone from home for awhile, and Bobbie was in school, Mr. Lincoln often took the boys to his office with him.

He would be so absorbed in work that the uninhibited youngsters would pull the books off the shelves, scatter the legal documents, ruin pens, and spill ink all over the place, much to the disgust of their father's junior law partner, Billy Herndon. He said if they were his kids, he would wring their little necks. Lincoln would just laugh. He accepted it as natural behavior for little boys. If they did something really bad, then he could talk the matter over with them until they saw why it was wrong.

That junior law partner, William Herndon, caused Mary and her husband much grief. He was always getting drunk and causing disturbances. Mr. Lincoln gave a lot of his own money to bail him out of jail. He also paid many bad debts for the man. Abe thought he could help Mr. Herndon to change. Mary did not approve of the drinking or the careless ways of Mr. Herndon and did not invite him to their home for fear of exposing the boys to his rudeness and bad habits.

A REMODLED HOME

Mr. Lincoln was becoming more prosperous and prominent and Mary decided to make her home even nicer for her family and more fitting for an up-and-coming lawyer and politician. She had inherited enough money from her father's will to pay for the remodeling. Lincoln fully agreed she could handle the details. During the remodeling, he was called away to conduct some urgent business on the law circuit.

The home was expanded, the roof was raised, and the little cottage turned into a stately two-story house. When Mr. Lincoln returned from this extended trip, he saw the beautiful finished product. Confused, he asked a boy on the street, "Could you direct me to Mr. A. Lincoln's house?"

At that moment, three boys jumped from their hiding place behind the fence. Bobbie, Willie and Tad all shouted: "Surprise! Pa! This IS your house." Abe gathered the boys around him and they hurried to the front door to hug their Mother.

The News of Mr. Lincoln's return spread like wildfire. Soon the house was filled with friends, associates, and even the well-paid craftsmen who had helped to pull this surprise off.

The boys said their Pa's grin was as wide as the Mississippi River when he saw the new bedrooms upstairs.

HOW TO STOP SLAVERY

Lincoln met many people in his travels throughout the state. The many court houses on the circuit welcomed him for his fairness, knowledge of the law and decisive manner in which he presented his clients' cases. He was successful in representing them with fairness and accuracy with regard to the laws. He treated everyone with respect and they respected him in return. He had been fair and honest as their congressman and the word was getting around that Lincoln was the man to stop slavery.

In 1855, encouraged by others, Lincoln once again became interested in politics because everyone in the country was talking about slavery. The northern states said there should be no slaves. The South declared they needed to have slaves to work their big plantations and claimed their economy couldn't survive without them.

Abraham Lincoln spoke out against slavery. He had many debates with a man named Stephen A. Douglas who argued in favor of slavery. Lincoln condemned slavery as a "moral, social and political evil."

Mr. Douglas had once been one of Mary's beaus. She had chosen Abe Lincoln over him and she still felt Abe could win any thing over Mr. Douglas, especially in the matter of slavery, because she shared the belief that slaves should be freed.

Lincoln did not win his bid for the U. S. Senate seat against Mr. Douglas, but people all over the country were now beginning to hear about Abraham Lincoln.

There was terrible trouble in the country. If they were not going to be allowed to keep their slaves, the states in the southern part of the U.S.A. said they were going to secede, or split from the northern states. People all over the land hoped Abraham Lincoln could save the country from being divided.

Abraham Lincoln won the election for the highest office in the land, the President of the United States of America, just at a time when the states weren't *united* at all.

The United States Flag had 33 stars and 13 stripes when Lincoln became president. He wanted it to stay that way; he desperately wanted to save the union.

*M*ary with her sons Willie and Tad in Springfield, in a photograph taken shortly after Lincoln's election in 1860. Credit: Courtesy of the Illinois State Historical Library.

Pageant of Politics

Political procession in summer of 1860. Lincoln in light suit is standing by the front door. The picture captured everything: the parade going by the Lincoln home, the waving hats, the unkempt small-town surroundings, the figures in the upper windows, everything except the loud hurrahs.

LINCOLN BIDS HIS SPRINGFIELD FRIENDS FAREWELL

Hundreds of the Lincoln's friends and neighbors stood at the Springfield railroad depot on the cold and dismal morning of February 11, 1861. From the back of the train, Abe looked out at a sea of faces and black umbrellas. His long fingers stroked the new beard that framed his sad face as he said goodbye.

"My friends . . . to this place, and the kindness of these people, I owe everything. Here I have lived a quarter of a century, and have passed from a young to an old man. Here my children have been born, and one is buried.

I now leave, not knowing when, or whether ever, I may return, with a task before me greater than that which rested upon Washington. Without the assistance of that Divine Being, who ever attended him, I cannot succeed. With that assistance, I cannot fail . . . . To His care commending you, as I hope in your prayers you will commend me, I bid you an affectionate farewell."

A NEW "FIRST LADY" AND PRESIDENT
OF THE UNITED STATES

"Mrs. President" in a
formal portrait taken by
Mathew Brady in 1861.
Credit: The Ostendorf Collection.

President Lincoln in a
portrait taken by Mathew
Brady, probably in 1863.
Credit: The Library of Congress.

When Abraham Lincoln won the election to the highest office in the United States, Mary found herself in the role of "First Lady" and lived up to the task.

She entertained graciously, remembering the manners and social graces she had learned so well in school. The President's wife treated all the guests with respect. She cared about them all.

It was the style for women to wear big hooped skirts in 1862. Mary loved to dress in beautiful satin or velvet dresses and hoped to make President Lincoln proud of his wife.

THE FIRST FAMILY

Lincoln's Family included, left to right, Mrs. Mary Todd Lincoln and their sons, William Wallace (Willie), Robert Todd, and Thomas (Tad). Robert was away at college during most of Lincoln's presidency.

Library of Congress

The Lincolns found the White House deplorably run down when they moved in. The furniture was ramshackle and shabby. Congress voted money for renovation and redecorating and Mary had the eye, the ability, and desire to oversee the restoration that first year in the White House. She shopped in Philadelphia and New York and was happy with the improvements . . . especially the installation of modern conveniences such as gas and water. The First Lady wanted the country to be proud of its heritage and the White House was a symbol of that heritage. She felt a responsibility to leave the Mansion in the best condition possible as it belonged to all the country and any citizen or visitor should feel welcome there.

Ben Perley Poore, an experienced journalist and observer who knew Washington affairs wrote:

> *"I am sure that since the time that Mrs. Madison presided at the White House, it has not been graced by a lady as well fitted by nature and by education to dispense its hospitalities as is Mrs. Lincoln. Her hospitality is only equaled by her charity and her graceful deportment by her goodness of heart."*

But many newspapers and a growing number of people in America criticized her for spending too much money.

FRIENDS FOR WILLIE AND TAD

The Lincolns' oldest son, Robert, was seldom in the White House because he was attending Harvard University but was home to Willie and Tad. Their mother was concerned that they were lonely and not having any fun. She hired good private tutors for her sons, but the boys needed friends.

But that would change when Julia Taft, 16-year-old daughter of Horatio N. Taft, a prominent Washington judge, visited the White House and mentioned her two younger brothers. Willie was going-on-eleven and Tad nearly eight at this time. Julia's two younger brothers, "Bud" and "Holly," were approximately the same ages.

As soon as Mrs. Lincoln found out about the brothers, she said to Mrs. Taft: "Send Bud and Holly around tomorrow, please. Willie and Tad are so lonely and everything is strange to them here in Washington." Mary had tried constantly to keep life in the White House normal and happy for the children.

They became favorite visitors and frequent accomplices in the mischief of the Lincoln boys. From that time on, the four irrepressible little boys romped through and threatened demolition of the Executive Mansion and the Taft home, visiting back and forth and eating meals indiscriminately at either place. Bud was Willie's crony and Holly was Tad's. It was Julia's dubious privilege to look after the four boys for nearly a year. Mrs. Lincoln and Julia spent much time talking to each other, confiding in each other. Perhaps Mary felt that this bright young woman was the daughter she'd never have. Julia was very accomplished on the piano but only the First Lady could succeed in getting her to play while she turned the pages for her.

LET THE CHILDREN HAVE A GOOD TIME

Julia learned that the motto of the Lincolns was "Oh, just let the children have a good time." Julia told Mary that when she entered a chamber she beheld the President lying on the floor with four boys on top, trying to hold him down.

One night, when Bud and Holly Taft stayed at the White House because it was raining too hard for them to go home, Mrs. Lincoln dressed the four boys in fresh shirts and let them attend a state dinner, sitting near the foot of the table. When Mrs. Taft heard of it, she disapproved, evidently not believing that "letting the children have a good time" was quite as important as that.

Once while Mrs. Lincoln was visiting with Julia, and doing nice things for her, she failed to notice the mischievous boys had gone missing. Their playful minds had planned an attack on an important meeting the President was having with his military advisors. The boys opened the door and pushed the barrel of a toy canon through and fired! Confetti bullets clouded the room. Lincoln and the men laughed while Mary quickly apologized and pulled the perpetrators from the room.

The adventures of Willie and Tad in the White House were legion and legend. Both Lincoln parents held the somewhat Western viewpoint that pranks were funny; and both, on occasion, had been guilty of prankish jokes themselves. The White House had to take a lot of romping-clattering from the little imps who raced from roof to basement, and turned it into a war zone playhouse.

A CIRCUS IN THE ATTIC!

The mansion roof took on various capacities. It was circus grounds (admission five cents for white or colored, the boys being as fair as their parents). Willie wrote many show scripts and kept lots of notebooks. He had written the circus program they performed with the help of the Taft brothers, Halsey (called Holly) and Bud. Tad flew out from behind the stage curtain—two sheets the boys had pinned together.

"Come help, Julie," he cried when the Taft brothers' sister came up to the circus. We're having a circus and my face has got to be blacked up and Willie can't get his dress on and Bud's bonnet won't fit."

They were practicing a song that Julie didn't think was complimentary to the president, but was popular—"Old Abe Lincoln Came out of the Wilderness."

Julie cried, "Boys does the President know about this?"

Tad nodded. "Pa knows and he won't care neither. He's coming up when those generals go away," he said, showing her a copy of the "official program" Willie had made.

The President of the United States attended the circus up in the attic of the White House after an important meeting. He was admitted only after paying the five cents for the privilege and a special reserved seat.

Tad held out a hat for the admission charge from a crowd of soldiers, sailors, gardeners, and his mother who crept in quietly with the cook. Mary couldn't wait to see Willie in the dress he had taken out of her closet.

Then Tad introduced the play. It lasted nearly an hour. President Lincoln "threw back his head and laughed heartily." The audience laughed loudly through the play from the beginning to its conclusion. Mary moved to her husband's side, giggling herself. Lincoln pulled her to his lap, still shaking from laughter. He kissed her cheek and could hardly stop laughing as he confided,

"I paid the 5 cents but it was worth at least a gold coin."

GIFTS TO THE PRESIDENT'S SONS

Many pets were given to the two boys—dogs, ponies, goats—

Willie had a pony that he regularly rode around the White House lawns. One night he had come in soaking wet as he had ridden the pony in a downpour.

But of all Willie and Tad's pets, their favorites were two small goats, Nanko and Nanny. The goats had the run of the White House, tearing up the gardens and sleeping on the boys beds. Tad harnessed Nanko to a kitchen chair and, using it like a sled, scuttled through the East Room scaring many fine ladies in their hooped skirts and finery.

President Lincoln wrote to Mary while she vacationed with Tad in New York. "Tell dear Tad, poor 'Nanny Goat' is lost. The day you left, Nanny was found resting herself, and chewing her little cud on the middle of Tad's bed. But now she is gone . . . and has not been heard of since. This is the last we know of poor Nanny." [A copy of this letter has been saved.]

The goats had a mysterious end, thanks to the housekeeper and the gardener who had enough of the flowers being eaten on the White House grounds.

Once again the Washington press was on the attack. There were many publicized and exaggerated incidents about all the antics of the Lincoln boys. Mary was highly criticized for letting them run wild and free in the halls of the White House.

Robert, the Lincoln's oldest son, had grown to manhood. He visited the White House often and drew closer to his mother because of a romance that was in the making for him and Mary Harlan, a senator's attractive daughter. The Lincoln's approved of the match. The marriage was destined to take place three years later when Mary would give a Mother's loving heart to Robert's wife.

THE LINCOLNS ATTEND CHURCH

The First Lady believed in God.
With her family at her side she found peace at Church.

Mary had attended church regularly with her father and family as she grew up. After she married, Abe often attended with her. When they lived in the White House it was a weekly priority. Tad only went to be with Willie, who liked to go and was as "good as pie."

Tad wondered out loud, "Why do the preachers always pray so long for you, Pa?"

Lincoln's smile faded when he said, "I suppose it's because the preachers think I need it," and then half to himself added, "I guess I do."

WILLIE AND TAD

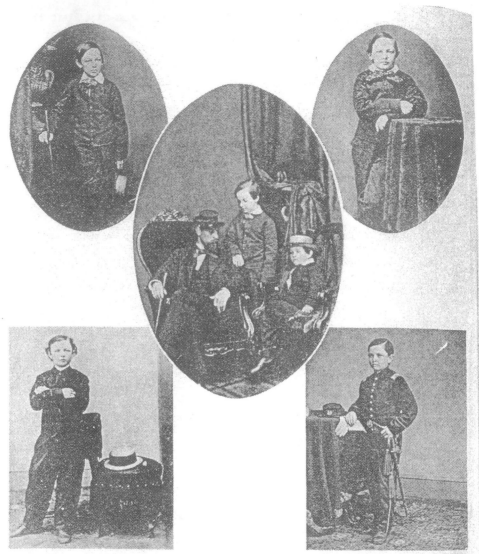

Willie and Tad

Upper left and right, Willie Lincoln; *lower left and right*, Tad Lincoln; *center*, Willie and Tad with Lockwood Todd, cousin of Mrs. Lincoln. These boys from "uncivilized" Illinois were a contrast to "the curled darlings of fashionable mothers" in Washington. Tad "in his gray trap-door pants, made, in true country style, to button to a waist" wanted to punch a boy who called him a "mud sill."

Willie made little speeches, wrote verses, and was said by all to be the counterpart of his father. Lincoln himself said Willie's mental processes were like his own.

GREATER SORROW

The noisy voices of little boys playing in the White House became suddenly subdued in February 1862 when Willie became ill. Besides his parents, he asked for his pal, Bud Taft, to be at his bedside. Willie's fever fluctuated. Mary stayed close to his side. For several weeks, she trembled with worry . . . praying for God, in the name of Jesus Christ, to heal him. Many doctors attended Willie constantly. On February 20, Willie had a momentary brightening and seemed to be getting better, but then, that evening the long struggle ended and his little form lay forever still. His parents held him, not wanting to let go. Then they clung to each other as their sorrow spilt over, their voices choked with pitiful sobs. They cried over and over, "We loved him so."

When eleven-year-old Willie died at the White House, the papers said he had been suffering from Bilious or Typhoid Fever. Mary had rallied from Eddie's death, but now she was mired in the midst of war, suspicion, criticism, slander and hate. It was more than she could bear.

Because Mary's family was from the South or the Confederate States, people accused her of being a "spy in the White House." They would not believe she was loyal to the North, the Union states. Criticism kept swirling around the country and gossip was rampant. Gossip and innuendo meant nothing to her now. All that mattered was that dearest Willie was gone—a greater sorrow, the loss of another son.

Mary could not accept that Willie had died. She could not stand up and be hostess for the White House functions. All parties and receptions were cancelled. The very people who criticized her for having too many parties, now condemned her for not having any. Lincoln too, could not stop grieving for this son, the one so like him, blessed with abilities much like his father. The president often went to visit Willie's tomb. He kept a picture of Willie on his desk and showed it along with a stack of Willie's notebooks to visitors. He also kept a Bible on his desk and often opened it for comfort and guidance.

Tad was lost in the emptiness around him. His big brother, who had always taken the lead, was not there to encourage him on. He clung to his "Pa" and President Lincoln took Tad everywhere with him, even letting him stay in the Oval Office while he worked. The poor little fellow would fall asleep under the desk and the weary President was often seen carrying him up to bed, sometimes late at night.

Courtesy of Frederick H. Meserve (for upper left) and of the National Archives

Oldest and Youngest of the Lincoln Boys

Robert is shown in two pictures *at the right.*
Upper left shows Lincoln with Tad. "The head of a great and powerful nation . . . soothing with loving care the little restless creature so much dearer than all the power he wields . . ." Stanton humored Tad by giving him an officer's commission (see *lower left*).

"A HOUSE DIVIDED AGAINST ITSELF CANNOT STAND."

These were the words of President Lincoln. He carried the weight of The Civil War on his mind and on his shoulders. This was the war where the Union Army of the northern states fought against slavery. The Confederate Army of the southern states fought to keep their slaves and that meant splitting the country in two. Abraham Lincoln knew he must keep this one nation, "under God," together if our country was to stay great.

Lincoln was dedicated to the proposition that ALL MEN ARE CREATED EQUAL, just as those men, the signers of the Declaration of Independence were, "four score and seven years ago . . ." (That means eighty-seven years.)

The First Lady tried to keep her mind off her grief and all the criticism that was thrown at her by visiting the hospitals to help and comfort the soldiers who had been wounded in the terrible Civil War. President Lincoln felt the sorrow of parents losing sons. He knew the ache families were suffering with the deaths of fathers, husbands, brothers and especially sons . . . millions of soldiers and brothers fighting to bring peace and freedom to a great country. President Lincoln visited many hospitals and battle grounds daily. He and Mary shed tears with the parents of the dying and wounded brave soldiers. Their hearts were broken too.

Mary's dressmaker, Lizzie Keckley, was loyal to her. Mary had befriended her, had paid her wages, and would not dine at restaurants which refused Lizzie because of her mixed race. Let it be known that Mary Lincoln was not ashamed to accompany this woman whose mother was an African slave and whose father was a white plantation owner. President Lincoln also showed great respect for all races. He had the privilege of meeting Harriet Beecher Stowe, author of Uncle Tom's Cabin, a book that by 1853 became an international best seller which, for hundreds of thousands of readers, dramatized the horrors of slavery.

The President greeted her and said,

"So this is the little lady who made this big war."

THE GETTYSBURG ADDRESS

Lincoln was a president who wrote his own speeches. This president didn't need speech writers. He was a genius at expressing a message needed to encourage and give hope to the nation. Lincoln spent many hours writing the document that freed the slaves: Then he delivered the Emancipation Proclamation. Today it is possible to get copies of his speeches over the internet . . . . a far advancement in technology which Lincoln never dreamed of as he wrote and rewrote by using a pen and paper.

After a Union victory at Gettysburg, Pennsylvania, Abraham Lincoln dedicated a cemetery there on November 19, 1863. He wrote the speech on the back of an envelope as he traveled on a train, with his wife and youngest son Tad, at his side. His speech took only two minutes. He wondered if it had been enough. [Today, it is one of the most memorized speeches in history.]

The Gettysburg Address

Four score and seven years ago our fathers brought forth on this continent a new nation, conceived in Liberty and dedicated to the proposition that all men are created equal.

Now we are engaged in a great Civil War, testing whether that nation, or any nation so conceived and so dedicated, can long endure. We are met on a great battle field of that war. We have come to dedicate a portion of that field, as a final resting place for those who here gave their lives that that this nation might live. It is altogether fitting and proper that we should do this.

But in a larger sense, we cannot dedicate—we cannot consecrate—we cannot hallow—-this ground. The brave men, living and dead, who struggled here, have consecrated it, far above our poor power to add or detract. The world will little note, nor long remember what we say here but it can never forget what they did here. It is for us the living, rather, to be here dedicated to the unfinished work which they who fought here have thus far so nobly advanced. It is rather for us to be here dedicated to the great task remaining before us—that from these honored dead we take increased devotion to that cause for which they gave the last full measure of devotion—that we here highly resolve that these dead shall not have died in vain—that this nation under God, shall have a new birth of freedom—and that government of the people, by the people, for the people, shall not perish from the earth.

THE CIVIL WAR WILL END

President Lincoln vowed the war would soon end and the country again be united. He dedicated his efforts to a peace treaty between generals and leaders to bring the Civil War to an end.

President Lincoln led the UNITED STATES through these events:
U.S. POPULATION WAS 32,351,000 in 1861.

Eleven Southern States, with over 9,000,000 persons
seceded from the Union.

West Virginia became a state in 1863, and Nevada in 1864.
Congress created the Arizona and Idaho territories in 1863, and the
Montana Territory in 1864

1861   **The Civil War began on April 12 when Confederate guns fired at Fort Sumter, a Union garrison in the harbor of Charleston, S.C.**

1862   **Congress created the Department of Agriculture.**

1863   **The first draft law in United States history, passed on March 3, gave the President authority to draft men from 20 to 45 for army service.**

1863   **President Lincoln delivered the Gettysburg Address on November 19.**

1864   **Lincoln was re-elected as President**

1865   **General Robert E. Lee surrendered his weary Confederate troops to General Ulysses S. Grant at Appomattox Court House on April 9**

ABRAHAM LINCOLN WAS ELECTED
FOR A SECOND TERM

After four long years, the Civil War ended in early April of 1865. President Lincoln worked hard to bring the country together. The people felt he was the only man who could save the nation and elected him again.

Many Northerners wanted to make the Southerners pay for the four terrible years of war. Some Southerners wanted revenge for their terrible defeat.

In his second inaugural address President Lincoln explained that the southern states should be taken back into the Union without hatred and cruelty and with forgiveness.

These last words of his second Inaugural Address, deemed by many to be his greatest, helped bring the country together . . .

"WITH MALICE TOWARD NONE
WITH CHARITY FOR ALL"

APRIL 14, 1865

Five days after the end of the Civil War, President Lincoln rose early and was in his office by his usual seven in the morning. It was Good Friday, April 14, 1865.

That morning, Mr. Lincoln ate breakfast with his family. His eldest son, Robert, a junior officer on General Grant's staff, was home from the war. The President was eager to hear Robert's report as he had been at Appomattox when Lee surrendered. The report from General Ulysses S. Grant was to be an important part of the cabinet meeting to be held later that morning. President Lincoln wanted to hear the details first from his son and to spend some time with him.

At the Cabinet meeting, Lincoln was jubilant. General Grant described his final drive of the war and gave details of General Lee's surrender just five days before. Lincoln spoke kindly of Lee and other Confederate officers. He said he hoped there would be no persecutions, "no bloody work, because enough blood had already been shed."

After lunch, Lincoln signed a pardon for a deserter saying, "The boy can do us more good above ground than underground." He also revoked the death sentence of a Confederate spy.

Lincoln sent a note to the First Lady to remind her that by four in the afternoon, he would escape from his office to take her for a quiet drive as he often did to be alone with her. They talked of their life ahead. He put his arm around Mary, and said, "We must both be more cheerful in the future. This war and the loss of our darling Willie have made us both very miserable." The talk they had made them feel so close. Mary was unwilling to be away from him. Even though she had not felt like going out, she agreed to attend Ford's Theatre production of the comedy, "An American Cousin" that night, because Lincoln thought a good laugh might help them both.

AT FORD'S THEATRE—APRIL 14, 1865

The President and his wife had invited guests, Miss Clara Harris and her fiancé, Major Henry R. Rathbone, to accompany them. After a standing ovation from the crowd, the two couples sat down to enjoy the play. The story continued on as they sat in the flag-draped box at Ford's Theater, the president in a large rocking chair, Mary at his side. During the third act, Mary was nestled against her husband. She glanced at their guests and then looked up into her husband's face and asked, "What will Miss Harris think of my hanging on to you so?"

"She won't think anything about it," he answered, giving her an affectionate smile as he held his wife's hand close in his own.

Lincoln was enjoying the play immensely while his wife was holding his hand, leaning close to him. Behind them, the door to the presidential box was closed but not locked. Lincoln's bodyguard that evening, John Parker, had slipped away from his post outside the door to go downstairs and watch the play.

A CONSPIRACY UNFOLDS

During the third act of the play, a few minutes after ten o'clock . . . . a premeditated evil, planned by disgruntled scoundrels from the Confederate states, was carried out. The leader of the conspirators was a murderous actor from the south who knew the very moment in the play when his shot could be concealed . . . the exact time to assassinate the president . . . . while the other conspirators would murder selected Union leaders at specified places . . . at the appointed time: ten p.m.! The moment to fulfill the plot to commit the most hideous crime in the country's history had come. It was at a high point of audience laughter . . . when a shadowy figure stepped through the unguarded door to the President's box . . . stretched out his arm, aimed a small derringer pistol at the back of Lincoln's head, and pulled the trigger !

But the audience laughter didn't cover the shot that rang out through the crowded playhouse. Major Rathbone lunged at the gunman making him drop the smoking pistol, but the traitor responded by yelling some curse and swinging a hunting knife in his left hand, slashing the Major's arm to the bone. Mary fell on the President. She held her husband back from sliding from his chair.

Women were screaming "THE PRESIDENT HAS BEEN SHOT!!!" Major Rathbone was shouting, "Catch him . . . Stop him!" while at the same time the guilty assassin was waving his bloody dagger and jumping from the President's box to the stage, twelve feet below. As he fell, the spur of his boot caught in the American Flag draped over the box. The actors on stage heard the bone in the fleeing man's left leg snap. Some ran toward him—recognizing the assailant as John Wilkes Booth, a self-glorified actor. The killer was faltering, staggering . . . threatening the actors with his bloody knife. He seized his greatest dramatic stage moment as he shouted an oath to the audience: "Sic simper tyrannis." (Latin for "Thus it shall ever be for tyrants.")

He still waved his bloody knife as he limped to the door at the back of the stage, crashed through the exit where a boy was holding the saddled horse that this crazed man had rented. The murderer grabbed the reigns with his free hand, then kicked the boy with his right foot, knocking him to the ground, and raced away into the night, looking for the other conspirators. Their assassination attempts had failed . . . unbeknownst to Booth. Other hateful men aided him in a 12-day flight from his pursuers. It ended in a burning barn where the evil John Wilkes Booth showed no remorse. He was shot trying to defend himself. Others who assisted in his escape were later captured and hanged for their treacherous acts of conspiracy.

THE GREATEST SORROW

Meanwhile, Mary was at the bleeding president's side, full of grief and panic. She covered his unconscious face with kisses, calling him every endearing name and begging him to speak just one word to her. But it was to no avail. He was not to speak again to her or to anyone. Someone got the word to a children's theatre where Tad was with many of his friends. Tad screamed when the news was announced and was quickly taken to his Pa's side to be with his Mother.

The best doctors were summoned but it was evident that the President was dying. They chose to move him to a better place—the Petersen House across the street. Here more doctors frantically attended to him. Mary did not want to leave him but she and Tad had to move aside so the doctors could work. President Lincoln's breathing stopped at 7:20 the next morning.

The whole world grieved when Abraham Lincoln died. His funeral was held in the East Room of the White House on April 19. After the service, a long procession, led by a detachment of black troops, moved slowly up Pennsylvania Avenue to the muffled beat of drums and the tolling of church bells. When they reached the Capitol Building, Lincoln's coffin was carried inside where he lay in state under the huge dome. Thousands of people, black and white, soldiers and civilians, old and young, stood patiently in the rain, waiting to file past the open coffin.

Mary insisted that Lincoln's body be enclosed in a Tomb at Oak Ridge Cemetery in Springfield, Illinois where his two sons, Eddie and Willie could be moved to rest beside him. Willie's body was taken from the tomb in Washington D.C. to travel by train next to his father's casket.

April 21, a black-draped funeral train set out to carry Lincoln's body across America back to his home, stopping at many cities where thousands of people crowded to pay their respects to a great President.

The morning of May 3, 1865 the train finally reached its destination at the Springfield train station where regiments of soldiers and delegations of officials were waiting. Tens of thousands of people jammed the streets around the station. Others stood on nearby rooftops. A military band played a funeral dirge. All the bells tolled. Guns fired a salute. The crowd fell silent as the train came to a stop, the train that carried home this great President who had saved the union of the United States of America.

RUMORS, LIES, GOSSIP—MONEY FOR WRITERS

After famous men and women die, many people wanting to make money, write stories, give sensational lectures and start scandalous rumors. This is what Mr. William Herndon did. He was the man who had once been Lincoln's law partner. Billie Herndon was disappointed that President Lincoln had not given him the appointment he sought in the U. S. government. Herndon thought Mary had influenced President Lincoln against him. For whatever reason, Mr. Herndon wrote mean and cruel things about Mary Todd Lincoln, stories that were not true. He wrote that Lincoln had never loved his wife, but had buried his heart with his childhood sweetheart when she died—a girl named Ann Rutledge. Mary became enraged. She had never even heard the name *Ann Rutledge* before. Abe had always told Mary that she was his only love.

The truth is that Mr. Lincoln had boarded at the Rutledge Tavern where Ann lived with her parents. Lincoln never courted Ann. She was engaged to another young man, who grieved greatly when she died. Herndon twisted the story and said it was Lincoln who had loved her and could not recover from her death. Many authors copying this story still write this same lie. Mr. Herndon told people in his lectures and stories that Mary was high-strung, spoiled and a mean, crude lady. All Herndon's tales were being printed in the newspapers. There were so many lies that Mary didn't know how to cope. Many of Mary's letters were preserved, proof of her ability to understand politics, support good men for office, proof of her ability to write intelligently . . . even as well as her husband, a master of the English language.

Mary's life was proof of her caring for fairness and her respect for others. She expressed great sorrow to others in their trials, even as she was trying to cope with the loss of two sons and a beloved husband. She had faith that Lincoln was with her two sons in heaven, a belief she could not forsake. All her life Mary had attended church. She believed in God and his son, Jesus Christ. She prayed and prayed daily. She was a brilliant, gracious woman who spoke her mind, but treated people with love and respect. She loved her husband and sons with a passion that most people do not display.

Even Mary's son, Robert, tried to get Herndon to stop his lies. Robert could not bear to see his Mother in so much anguish and humiliation. He was a loyal son who she could depend on to love and sympathize with her.

ATTEMPTS TO STOP LIES FAIL
THE PRESS FUELS ON

"To avoid persecution from the vampire press, I have decided to flee to a land of strangers." The land Mary chose was Germany. Mary was trying to support Tad in getting a good education and enrolled him in many good schools. Frankfurt was the place recommended for good schools for Tad. Mary was charmed by Frankfurt and stayed there for two years. There was plenty to do while Tad attended school. There was shopping and sightseeing and she even bumped into royalty. She visited spas that the doctors recommended would be good for her nerves and arthritis. Tad was given permission to take his dinner every night with his mother at her hotel and stay over as he wished. Tad had also taken many trips to other European countries with his mother, countries his father had planned to visit with her.

In 1871 the Lincolns returned to the United States. Mary might have settled permanently in Frankfurt, but Tad was "almost wild to see Robert," Mary confessed. She consented to return. A child had been born to Robert and his wife, another Lincoln baby, a girl named Mary. Nothing could have gladdened her heavy heart more.

Tad and his mother had a miserable voyage home—chilly winds for all eight days, and a severe storm in the mid-Atlantic. By the time they landed in New York, Tad had a heavy cough and a severe cold. Mary's arthritic joints ached.

The New York Times reported on their arrival: *"Mrs. Lincoln is delighted to be in her native land . . . Tad speaks English with a foreign accent. He has grown up a tall, fine-looking lad of 18, bearing resemblance to his father, but only a faint resemblance to the tricksy little sprite that visitors to the White House remember . . . "*

Tad had been twelve when his father died. He was kind like his father. He knew the value of a pleasant compliment to his mother's battered spirit. "My Mother is a great woman," he would say to her playfully. Through affection he could influence her where others failed. Once she laid aside her mourning garments, because it was Tad's birthday and he wished it.

That voyage, though rough, held sweet anticipations for Tad and his mother as they traveled to Chicago pulled by the magnet of a granddaughter. Tad was happy to see his brother, sister-in-law and especially his little niece. Mary was the happiest she had been in years when she held that precious baby, whose parents had chosen to name her Mary.

EVEN DARKER DAYS AHEAD

Mary and Tad settled into the Clifton House in Chicago. From the beginning of his mother's widowhood his tender spirit rose to her need of him. When he heard her sobbing in the depths of night, he went to her bedside to comfort her. Things had changed for a crying 12-year old when his father died. He was now quiet and gentle mannered. Tad had never recovered from the cold and cough he got on the stormy trip over the Atlantic. Mary had a special chair made for him so he could recline in a comfortable position to breathe. The doctors had given Mary hope that he would recover but his cough only got worse.

Robert said "Tad never complained but endured with marvelous fortitude."

Fate handed Mary another severe blow. July 15, 1871, the teenager's suffering ended. Mrs. Lincoln's loving son Tad, who had stood by his mother's side all these sad years, was dead.

The next day, a simple funeral was held in Robert's home. Friends, relatives, classmates—all came to pay their respects to the youngest son of Abraham Lincoln. Tad, too, was buried in the tomb with his beloved father and brothers in Springfield, Illinois.

A GRAND NEPHEW, EDWARD LEWIS BAKER, JR.

Mary's dear sister, Elizabeth and her husband, N. W. Edwards welcomed her to live at their home—which had happy memories for President Lincoln's widow. Their grandson, Edward Lewis Baker, Jr. reminded her of Willie and Tad. He through the next few years would take his aunt Mary to the departures and meet her on her returns when she visited other countries, especially France where her knowledge of the French language made her feel secure. The people there treated her with respect. Her great link to home was through constant letter-writing . . . especially to Lewis, this grand nephew who answered and saved all her letters . . . letters that were used by the author to whom this book is dedicated. Mary Lincoln was a talented writer and observer of people. She even kept track of politics in America by reading newspapers. When Mary returned to America, she continued writing letters to friends and family and even politicians.

Unfortunate for her—she was friendly to everyone, even telling her story to clerks in stores where she loved to shop. Unbeknown to the clerks, this widow shared many things which she bought in numbers . . . things like white gloves which she gave to anyone, especially ladies who admired them. She gave items of clothing to needy women who waved to her in her carriage. It did not make the news of Mary's compassion to poor women she saw in the streets whose crying babies were dressed in tatters, covered with worn blankets. Her carriage driver often took her to the underprivileged areas of town to leave baby clothes and bonnets for the women. They accepted with gratitude and respect to this old lady, who was a stranger in their streets. Many destitute women lingered on roads hoping that she would return . . . yet some remembered . . . told their tales long after Mary Todd Lincoln died . . . a missing tale of her kind acts.

Mary, typical of older people who are wont to reminisce, told her story to strangers hoping for a little understanding. Public opinion was so turned against her that people did not sympathize with her sad experiences. They thought she was eccentric. Some of her acquaintances thought she was insane to carry on so . . . thought she should be kept off the streets.

Good friends of President Lincoln's widow, Judge James Bradwell and his wife, Myra, immediately visited her and engaged several reliable doctors to give her thorough mental examinations. It was proven a false accusation. Mary Lincoln was NOT insane. Doctors found that her mind was not only clear, but highly intelligent.

RETURN
TO A HOME OF BEAUTIFUL MEMORIES

Mary's oldest sister Elizabeth and her husband, Mr. Edwards insisted and welcomed her to return and live with them again . . . in that same home where Abe had courted Mary.

The widow of President Lincoln was not well. On the afternoon of July 15, 1882 (the anniversary of Tad's death), Mary collapsed in her bedroom.

The next day, July 16, she died of a stroke.

It had been seventeen long, sad, tortured years after President Lincoln's death until his wife died in the friendly surroundings of her sister's home in Springfield, Illinois. Her supreme wish was now fulfilled: "to rest by the side of my darling husband."

Suddenly, Mary Lincoln was somebody again. The news of her death flashed over the country.

People streamed through the Edwards' parlor to get a final glimpse of the President's wife as she lay in her casket in the same room and almost the same place where forty years before she had stood as a bride.

A faint smile touched her lips
. . . and on her finger was a gold wedding band,
the one Abraham Lincoln had slipped on her finger so many years ago,
simply engraved,

LOVE IS ETERNAL.

APPENDIX

Ruth Painter Randall
(November 1, 1892 - January 22, 1971)

"At one minute after midnight, July 27, 1947 Mrs. Randall -- wife of J. G. Randall, our foremost Lincoln scholar, author of LINCOLN THE PRESIDENT, was present at the opening of the Lincoln Papers. In addition to consulting this original evidence, she made full use of the Herndon-Weik Papers. Mrs. Randall also had access to little-known manuscript collections and to private safe-deposit boxes which yielded letters never before used. The results of these researches is a biography which answers, once and for all, the charges leveled against Mary Lincoln for over a century and a half.

Carl Sandburg
(January 6, 1878 - July 22, 1967

Carl Sandburg was an American writer and editor, best known for his poetry. He won three Pulitzer Prizes, two for his poetry. His comments about Mrs. Randall's book, MARY LINCOLN, Biography of a Marriage are as follows:
"The most elaborately and scrupulously documented biography of Mary Lincoln, this is also the most keenly intuitive and sensitively written narrative of the days and years of the girl who became the wife and widow of Abraham Lincoln. It can stand as the first and most indispensable book to be read by those seeking to know about the domestic and connubial affairs, private and public, of the Lincoln couple. It is portraiture on an immense scale, winnows a harvest of hate, and moves often amid thickets of gossip, malice, and the willfully created misunderstanding that so often befog the American political scene."

Lincoln's Thanksgiving Proclamation

"I do, therefore, invite my fellow citizens in every part of the United States…to set apart and observe the last Thursday of November next as a day of Thanksgiving and Praise to our beneficent Father who dwelleth in the heavens…
[it is] announced in the holy Scriptures and proven by all history, that those nations are blessed whose God is the Lord…it has seemed to me fit and proper that God should be solemnly, reverently and gratefully acknowledged, as with one heart and one voice, by the whole American people."

On October 3, 1863, the Congress of the United States of America passed an Act designating an annual National Day of Thanksgiving…as proclaimed by President Lincoln.

"That I may proclaim with the voice of thanksgiving, and declare all thy wonders." Psalms 26:7

> As we remember the life of Abraham Lincoln and his wife, Mary, we give THANKS for their great compassion for others.

This majestic statue of Lincoln,
dominates the interior of the Lincoln Memorial.
Millions of people visit it every year.

The **Lincoln Memorial** is a beautiful monument in Washington, D.C., that honors Abraham Lincoln. It stands at the end of the Mall. It ranks as one of the most stately memorials of the 1900's The massive marble building is 188 feet long and 118 feet wide. It has a great hall surrounded by 36 Doric columns The columns stand for the 36 states in the Union when Lincoln was President. The outside decorations show the names of the 48 states that existed when the building was dedicated.

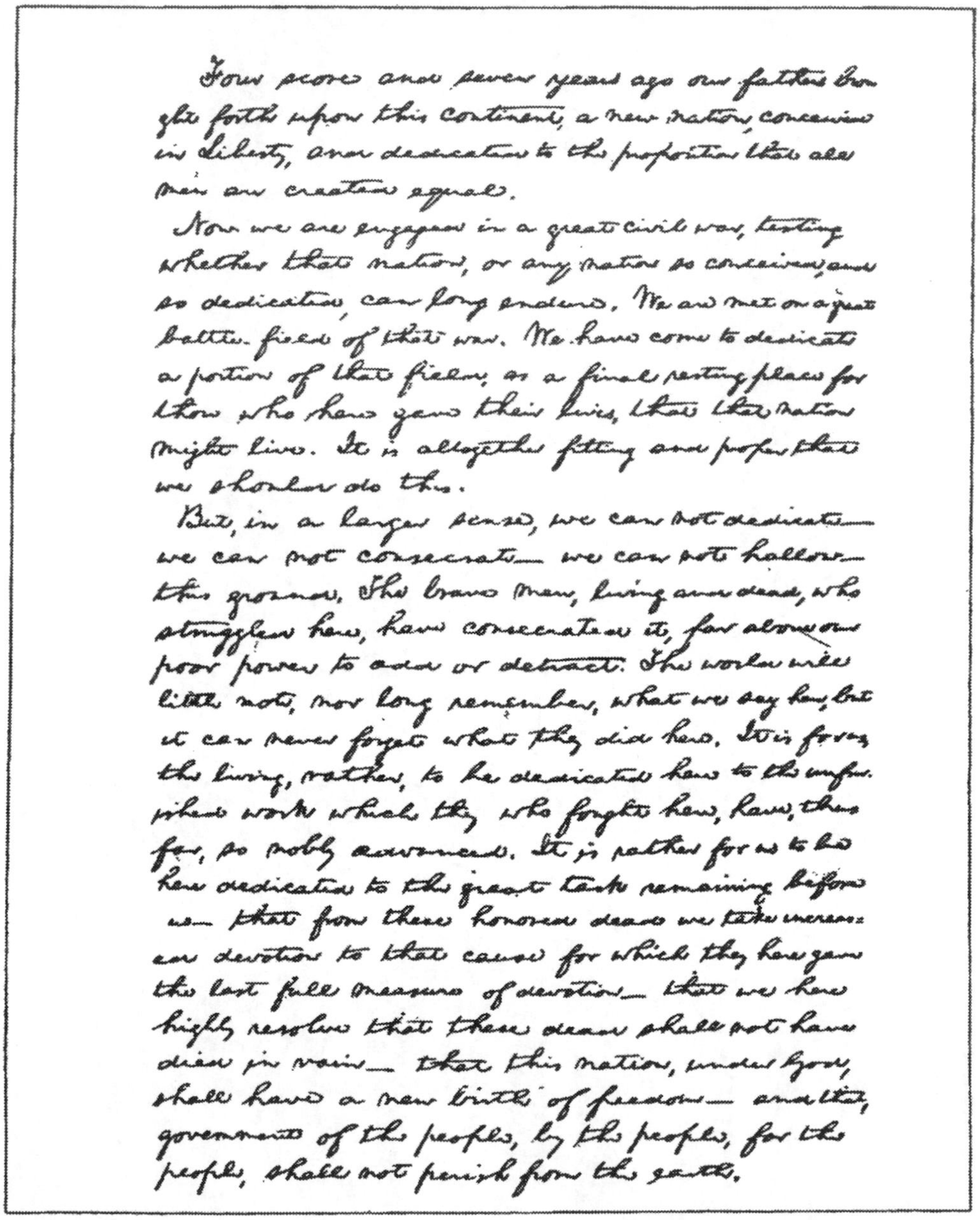

Lincoln wrote out six copies of the Gettysburg Address, and five are known to survive, all with slight differences. The copy shown here is on display at the Old State Capitol in Springfield.

The Gettysburg Address

**Gettysburg, Pennsylvania
November 19, 1863**

On June 1, 1865, Senator Charles Sumner commented on what is now considered the most famous speech by President Abraham Lincoln. In his eulogy on the slain president, he called it a "monumental act." He said Lincoln was mistaken that "the world will little note, nor long remember what we say here." Rather, the Bostonian remarked, "The world noted at once what he said, and will never cease to remember it. The battle itself was less important than the speech."

© Abraham Lincoln Online

Lincoln's second inaugural address

Abraham Lincoln delivered his **second inaugural address** on March 4, 1865, at the start of his second term as President of the United States. At a time when victory over the secessionists in the American Civil War was within days and slavery was near an end, Lincoln did not speak of happiness, but of sadness. Some see this speech as a defense of his pragmatic approach to Reconstruction, in which he sought to avoid harsh treatment of the defeated South by reminding his listeners of how wrong both sides had been in imagining what lay before them when the war began four years earlier.

Both **The Gettysburg Address and Lincoln's Second Inaugural Speech** are engraved on the walls of the Lincoln Memorial.

This photograph of Lincoln delivering his second inaugural address is the only known photograph of Lincoln giving a speech. Lincoln stands in the center, with papers in his hand. John Wilkes Booth is visible in the photograph, in the top row right of center

Abraham Lincoln

Second Inaugural Address

March 4, 1865

One of the great speeches of American history; some say, the greatest.

Fellow-Countrymen:

At this second appearing to take the oath of the Presidential office there is less occasion for an extended address than there was at the first. Then a statement somewhat in detail of a course to be pursued seemed fitting and proper. Now, at the expiration of four years, during which public declarations have been constantly called forth on every point and phase of the great contest which still absorbs the attention and engrosses the energies of the nation, little that is new could be presented. The progress of our arms, upon which all else chiefly depends, is as well known to the public as to myself, and it is, I trust, reasonably satisfactory and encouraging to all. With high hope for the future, no prediction in regard to it is ventured.

On the occasion corresponding to this four years ago all thoughts were anxiously directed to an impending civil war. All dreaded it, all sought to avert it. While the inaugural address was being delivered from this place, devoted altogether to saving the Union without war, urgent agents were in the city seeking to destroy it without war--seeking to dissolve the Union and divide effects by negotiation. Both parties deprecated war, but one of them would make war rather than let the nation survive, and the other would accept war rather than let it perish, and the war came.

One-eighth of the whole population were colored slaves, not distributed generally over the Union, but localized in the southern part of it. These slaves constituted a peculiar and powerful interest. All knew that this interest was somehow the cause of the war. To strengthen, perpetuate, and extend this interest was the object for which the insurgents would rend the

Union even by war, while the Government claimed no right to do more than to restrict the territorial enlargement of it. Neither party expected for the war the magnitude or the duration which it has already attained. Neither anticipated that the cause of the conflict might cease with or even before the conflict itself should cease. Each looked for an easier triumph, and a result less fundamental and astounding. Both read the same Bible and pray to the same God, and each invokes His aid against the other. It may seem strange that any men should dare to ask a just God's assistance in wringing their bread from the sweat of other men's faces, but let us judge not, that we be not judged. The prayers of both could not be answered. That of neither has been answered fully. The Almighty has His own purposes. "Woe unto the world because of offenses; for it must needs be that offenses come, but woe to that man by whom the offense cometh." If we shall suppose that American slavery is one of those offenses which, in the providence of God, must needs come, but which, having continued through His appointed time, He now wills to remove, and that He gives to both North and South this terrible war as the woe due to those by whom the offense came, shall we discern therein any departure from those divine attributes which the believers in a living God always ascribe to Him? Fondly do we hope, fervently do we pray, that this mighty scourge of war may speedily pass away. Yet, if God wills that it continue until all the wealth piled by the bondsman's two hundred and fifty years of unrequited toil shall be sunk, and until every drop of blood drawn with the lash shall be paid by another drawn with the sword, as was said three thousand years ago, so still it must be said "the judgments of the Lord are true and righteous altogether."

With malice toward none, with charity for all, with firmness in the right as God gives us to see the right, let us strive on to finish the work we are in, to bind up the nation's wounds, to care for him who shall have borne the battle and for his widow and his orphan, to do all which may achieve and cherish a just and lasting peace among ourselves and with all nations.

WHITE HOUSE

The White House is the official residence of the President of the United States.
The President lives and works in this world famous mansion in Washington D.C.
Mary Lincoln has been remembered as a "First Lady" who Congress voted
to oversee the renovation and decorating of a run down White House.
She is remembered more as a lady who presided at this national home
"well fitted by nature and by education to dispense its hospitalities.
Her charity and her graceful ways came from her goodness of heart."
The Lincoln sons were famous for their creative activities there.
Tragedy struck the first family.
Willie, sick with Typhoid Fever died in the White House.
Another tragedy hit the whole nation:
President Abraham Lincoln was assassinated.
He had seen the end of the Civil War; had united the country again.
The Lincolns days at the White House were over.

CREDITS

THE MISSING LINK ON MARY LINCOLN

was written by Anne G. Snow to teach boys and girls, their teachers and parents the truth about a great "First Lady," wife of President Abraham Lincoln.

Many books drag Mary through lies and gossip created by William Herndon. His false stories nearly destroyed Mary, but she did prevail and the truth will out. People still declare untruths about her. She was a highly intelligent and sane woman who deserves acceptance from all Americans.

This short book which compares Mary and Abe Lincoln from their births to their deaths was written to acquaint all readers with one of the greatest love stories in American history. The impressions the author had were strong to go on—not give up on a book first written many years ago. The best way to redeem Mary Lincoln could be a cover illustration that revealed Abe and Mary's immediate attraction to each other. Credit goes to SCOTT SNOW, Don and Anne's nephew, a successful artist. His illustration of Mary and Abe's first dance is a delight.

Bio: Anne Greaves Snow was born in Salt Lake City, on March 10, 1924; attended Columbus Elementary School during the Great Depression but remembers most her senior year at Granite High School when Pearl Harbor was bombed on Sunday, December 7, 1941. The next day, Monday, at school was surreal. Franklin D. Roosevelt, the four-term President declared war. All the men and eligible boys left for training in the Army or Navy. It was World War II. Women contributed to the War effort. Anne had a Civil Service job at the local ration board and like other patriotic Americans, wrote letters to many servicemen. After the long war she married Edward Donald Snow, a 6'4"handsome athlete who had played basketball for his High Schools and for BYU before he served four years in the 2nd Infantry Division. Don is a veteran of D-Day, the Battle of the Bulge, and fought in many campaigns throughout Europe.

They both graduated from BYU—Don in 1946 after WWII, and Anne in 1948. They were married in the Salt Lake Temple April 5, 1951. Both earned Master's Degrees. Don received his MS from BYU in 1954; Anne earned her MA at the University of Utah in 1977. The first decade of their married life, Don was head basketball coach at BY High, the laboratory school for BYU. While in Provo, three children were born to them: Edward, Cherie and Sarah. In 1959, Don was hired as head basketball coach at Granger, a new high school in Salt Lake County. Two more children, Randall and Wanda were born in Salt Lake City. All five children graduated from Granger High School where their father coached and taught. Anne taught elementary school, 5th and 6th grades and lastly ran a Media Center. After retirement they served a mission to Greece-Athens for: The Church of Jesus Christ of Latter-day Saints. They later retired to Provo, Utah.

It was a tradition for family members to join mother Anne's challenge to learn the Gettysburg Address when her Fifth graders were rewarded for doing the same. It was no surprise when Don repeated it to family members who visited him the day before he died, April 2, 2010, (Good Friday).

It is fitting that this book be further dedicated to

Don Snow

who encouraged his wife to share the truth about this famous American couple.